How to Write

Bar Exam Essays

Pass the Bar Exam Book Series

Book 1 – *Bar Exam Basics: A Roadmap to Bar Exam Success*

Book 2 – *How to Write Bar Exam Essays*

Book 3 – *Bar Exam Mind: A Strategy Guide for an Anxiety-Free Bar Exam*

Book 4 – *The Bar Exam Mind Bar Exam Journal*

Other bar exam resources available at BarExamMind.com

MBE Outlines

California Bar Outlines

101 Bar Exam Affirmations

Bar Exam Visualization Audio Program

How to Write

Bar Exam Essays:

Strategies and Tactics to Help You Pass the Bar Exam

Matt Racine

Editor, BarExamMind.com

Table of Contents

Introduction

Everyone seems to have one part of the bar exam that they dislike more than the others. For me, it was the MBE, while for some it is the performance test. But, based on surveys of my Bar Exam Mind blog readers, the majority of bar exam students have the most trouble writing bar exam essays.

In response to requests of my blog readers, I have written a few posts offering basic tips about bar exam essays, but I have never put together anything systematic. This book provides you with a systematic and uncomplicated approach to learn how to write passing bar exam essays.

In addition to being systematic, this book is also short. I made it short because the most important thing you can do to ensure you will pass the essay portion of the bar exam is to *practice writing essays*. This book will show you how to practice the right way, but the book cannot do the practice for you.

My intent is that you read this book in one or two sittings, and then begin to apply what you have read to your bar exam preparations.

This book explains the most important things to focus on so that you can make the most efficient use of your bar exam preparation time. The worst thing you can do while preparing for the bar exam is to spin your wheels wondering if you are doing the right things. That leads to frustration and anxiety.

With that in mind, this book begins with a chapter discussing the right mindset for bar exam preparation. It is important to have the right mindset so you can handle the inevitable highs and lows you will encounter while studying for the bar exam.

The next section of the book gets to the heart of the matter, discussing what I call the **four pillars** of bar exam essay writing: (1) technical requirements, (2) issue spotting, (3) outlining and formatting and (4) analysis. Each pillar has its own chapter, complete with examples.

After this, the book gives you a practice strategy and schedule to ensure that your practice time is well spent. I have included a link to a printable version of the schedule and an essay practice checklist to help you master the steps for essay writing. You can follow this method to the letter or use it as a basis for creating a practice method that works best for you.

In the end, what matters most for your essay practice is that you include time for *review* and *self-assessment*. If you simply blast through practice essay after practice essay, you will not learn nearly as much as if you take the time to spot your mistakes or weaknesses and learn from them.

The next chapter contains various tips and techniques I developed while taking and passing two bar exams. These tips will give you an advantage over your fellow bar exam takers.

The final chapter contains a strategy for use during the bar exam itself to maximize your scoring on the bar exam. It is simple to apply, but I have never seen anyone else mention it.

Let's get started.

Mindset for Essay Studying

Before we get into the nuts and bolts of writing a great bar exam essay, I need to say a few words about your studying mindset.

It is my opinion that mindset is a huge part of bar exam success. The creation of a success mindset is the basis for my Bar Exam Mind blog and my book, *Bar Exam Mind: A Strategy Guide for an Anxiety-Free Bar Exam*.

The genesis for this chapter was statements by people just like you who were complaining about how poorly they felt they were doing on their initial practice essays. They told me they felt frustrated and hopeless, fearing that they would never be able to pass the bar exam.

I'll just say right up front: It is *completely normal* to write some stinkers when you first start practicing. I can remember my first practice essays. They were so terrible I was convinced I would never be able to pass the bar exam.

Look, it is a well-known fact that many (most?) law students are perfectionists. They have a hard time with failure, even when that "failure" is meaningless in the grand scheme of life. Often, they think that they are stupid if they cannot learn something quickly. They get depressed for the simple fact that something takes more effort than they might be used to giving.

For most people, and I was no exception, studying for the bar exam is a tedious process. It is filled with moments of intense frustration and even anger. But, if you study consistently, working through these down moments, you will be able to learn more than enough to pass the bar exam.

Let's explore this a little more deeply as it relates to writing bar exam essays.

Growth vs. Fixed mindset

Carol Dweck, a world-renowned psychologist at Stanford University, has determined through decades of research on success and achievement that there are two general categories of mindset: fixed and growth.

A **fixed mindset** is much like what you would expect. With a fixed mindset, one believes one's basic qualities, like talent, intelligence or ability in a particular area, are simply fixed traits. Such people spend their time *documenting* their talent or intelligence instead of striving to develop them. They also believe (wrongly) that talent by itself creates success without effort.

I see the fixed mindset often in law students. Most of them have been good students throughout their lives, and many attribute this to their inborn talent and intelligence. They believe they are "smarter" than the average person and have excelled academically because of that superiority. When they have trouble academically or as they study for the bar exam, they tell themselves they are "stupid" or "won't ever get this stuff."

Contrast this to people with a **growth mindset.** Someone with a growth mindset believes his or her most basic abilities can be developed through hard work, dedication and perseverance. Intelligence and talent are a good foundation, but not nearly enough. People with a growth mindset tend to have much greater resilience and can endure more trying times and hardship to reach their goals.

If you do not have a growth mindset, be alert for negative self-talk about being too stupid to learn a particular concept or incapable of learning how to write a bar exam essay. These are the expressions of a fixed mindset. You need to instill in yourself a growth mindset as best as possible.

As a long-time victim of a fixed mindset, I know how self-criticism can push you into a dark place. It takes constant vigilance to remain in the light of a growth mindset.

When you recognize that your fixed mindset is belittling you, tell yourself that you are working hard and will soon learn what you need to learn. Replace any negative talk with positive statements or recall a time you worked hard for something and achieved a goal. It need not be an academic moment, but maybe some sport, skill or hobby you enjoy.

As recommended in *Bar Exam Mind,* you can also try using positive affirmations such as:

- I am relaxed and calm.

- My mind stores and recalls information with ease.

- My brain is healthy and efficient.

- I deserve success and happiness.

- I study for the bar exam easily and effortlessly.

Baby mind

It is my decidedly untrained and unscientific opinion that we are all born with a growth mindset. It is only later that it becomes fixed. If you don't believe me, think about how a baby learns to walk.

The baby looks around for a few months and sees everyone standing on two legs. The baby realizes that the best he or she can do is crawl. Eventually, the baby gets fed up with this state of affairs, and tries to walk but promptly falls down. Maybe the baby even cries, maybe the baby even gets hurt.

Does the baby give up?

No, the baby keeps trying.

Eventually, the baby can stand and walk, but is unsteady. After a few months, the baby confidently walks. By the time the child is three, it usually can walk and run very competently, sometimes even better than adults.

Imagine if the baby had a fixed mindset and stopped trying to walk the first time it fell and landed hard on its butt. There would be lots of crawling adults.

Failure in baby steps

For me, learning to write bar exam essays well is reminiscent of how babies learn to walk. Although I could already write when I started studying for the bar exam, I had no experience writing "bar exam style" essays.

I was used to writing expansive essays for law school exams, filled with things besides law and factual analysis. Things like policy arguments or debating the relative societal benefit of the rules of law in different jurisdictions.

All that is out the window when writing a bar exam essay.

The jurisdiction where I first took a bar exam (Oregon) had a length limit for typed essays of 4,000 characters. That's about one, single-spaced page. I remember thinking at the time, "How can I possibly fit a complete answer into such limited space?"

Adjusting to those restrictions was like learning an entirely new skill. I had to fail *a lot* before I gained rudimentary competence, and it took even more failures before I could consider myself "good" at writing a bar exam essay within the space of a mere 4,000 characters.

Learning

The process of learning to write bar exam essays well involves various steps, which we will discuss in the remainder of the book. For now, it is enough to understand you will need to write many practice essays in order to master the ability to write bar exam essays under the time pressure of the bar exam.

The actual number of practice essays necessary to perfect your skills will vary by student, but will certainly be more than just three or four. I estimate that I wrote at least 50 practice essays for my first bar exam, and at least 25 when I was studying for my second bar exam.

As previously mentioned, your initial essays will without doubt be subpar. When you compare them to model bar essay answers, you may be frustrated, depressed or even scared.

The important thing to do as you begin your essay practice is to analyze what went wrong, pick yourself up, and try again and again.

Conclusion

The early stages of bar prep can be hard on your self-confidence. This is true with MBE and performance test preparations, as much as with essay preparation.

The important thing is to believe in yourself, accept the little failures, learn from them, and keep moving forward.

If you would like a more systematic approach to developing your bar exam mindset, be sure to read my other book: *Bar Exam Mind: A Strategy Guide for an Anxiety-Free Bar Exam.*

First Things First

Before we begin our journey to learn how to write great bar exam essay responses, we need to know two things. First, we need to understand the parts of an essay question so we understand each other as we discuss them. Second, we need to review some sample answers so that we can understand what the graders believe is a good response.

Parts of an essay question

There are two main parts of an essay question: the fact pattern and the call of the question. Because you have been to law school, you should know all about these parts.

The fact pattern is simply the factual narrative given to you as the basis for your legal analysis. The call of the question is simply the analytical task or tasks given to you by the essay author. In other words, the call of the question directs your analysis. (More on the call of the question in a following chapter.)

Model essay answers

One of the best ways to master a new skill is to watch someone else perform the skill. When you see something done in front of your eyes, you not only know that it is truly possible, but you might pick up some hints about how to do it yourself.

With bar exam essays, the best way to recreate this process is reading some sample questions and answers. So, that is what I want you to do right now.

Action Step: Stop reading and get on the internet. Go to your jurisdiction's bar website and find some sample questions and answers from prior bar exams. If you can't find any on your state's bar website, you can use the sample answers included with your bar prep materials or you can get sample answers from the California, New York or Pennsylvania bar websites.

Find the most recent exam available and read *at least* two of the questions and answers. Even better, read all the questions and answers for one entire bar exam. This is likely to be between six and nine questions and responses. It may take some time, but it will be worth it.

As you read through these examples, note the way things are phrased, the use of headings (if any) and emphasis markings (e.g., **bold**, *italic*, underline), and the detail (or lack of it) in the analysis. Do not spend a ton of time on this. Just read through the questions and answers, getting a feel for how these model responses are structured.

Once you have read these samples, you know what you are shooting for. Just keep in mind that sometimes the sample answers posted on bar websites are nearly perfect, and far better than necessary to pass the bar exam. So, don't let this exercise discourage you. It is simply meant to give you a general understanding of what a bar exam essay response looks like.

Conclusion

Now that you know what typical bar exam essay questions and answers look like, we will break down the writing process. To do this, we need to discuss the four pillars of bar exam essay writing.

Four Pillars of Bar Exam Essay Writing

There are four things you need to master when studying for bar exam essays:

(1) technical requirements,

(2) issue spotting,

(3) outlining and formatting, and

(4) analysis.

The first step to mastering these four pillars is understanding *why* you need to master them. The second step is to *practice* the four pillars until you have mastered them.

Each of these four pillars will be discussed in more detail in the remainder of this book, but I'll give you a summary here so you know what you are in for.

Pillar 1: Technical requirements: timing, length, value

Timing matters because you must be able to read and respond to each essay question within the time given to you. If you are unable to do this, then it is likely you will spend too much time on one essay and fail to answer others.

The bar exam is pass/fail. You do not need to write spectacular essays to pass, but you do need to respond to all of them and write something competent.

The length requirements matter because they are a component of timing. If you are given a limited space in which to put your response, then it will affect how detailed your response can be. The shorter the maximum length allowed for each essay, the less detail you need to write.

And, it is important to know the value each essay is worth to your overall grade. If you are taking the bar exam in a jurisdiction where the essays are worth 30 percent, you might be able to get away with studying less than if you are in a jurisdiction where they count for 50 percent or more of your final score.

Pillar 2: Issue spotting

If you cannot analyze the fact pattern and figure out what the bar examiners want you to write about, then you simply will not be able to pass the essay portion of the bar exam. You must be able to spot the issues.

Pillar 3: Outlining and formatting

By formatting, I mean how to organize your essay response, and when to use headings or underlining in your response to direct the attention of the essay grader to critical points. This is important, but also pretty easy to figure out.

Also encompassed within the formatting pillar is creating an outline for your essay response prior to writing. Many students have trouble creating an essay outline. This is a problem because it increases the odds that the student will miss issues or leave out portions –

sometimes substantial portions – of the required analysis.

Pillar 4: Analysis

I have saved the best and most important thing for last. As you will recall from law school, there is usually not any certainty when responding to a law school essay question. There are usually facts or theories supporting both sides of an argument, such as a finding of liability versus one of no liability. The point is that you are being tested on how you interpret facts in light of the law, not how well you argue a single position.

It is typically the same in the bar exam. You will find yourself using phrases like "it is likely that a court

27

would find x, but it is also possible that defendant will prevail because of the affirmative defense of y" and "under these facts, it is not likely a court would find a contract was formed, but if it were formed, then Mr. D breached the contract when he did x, y and z."

Conclusion

With this short introduction in mind, let's turn to a more detailed discussion of each of the four pillars.

Pillar No. 1: Technical Requirements

You should not begin any essay practice until you understand the technical requirements of the essay portion of the bar exam as established by your jurisdiction. To do so would be like playing football without knowing the rules of the game or even where the boundary and goal lines are.

The applicable technical requirements can vary significantly by jurisdiction. And, depending on what those technical requirements are, they will affect how you will write your essays and how you will need to practice bar exam essays in order to be able to master them.

In jurisdictions with short time and length requirements, your essays will be more about issue spotting and rule statements. In jurisdictions allowing more time and space to write a response, you will need to increase the depth of your legal analysis.

For example, when I took the Oregon bar exam, I was given thirty minutes per essay and was assigned nine essays. Thirty minutes is not a lot of time to digest a 200- to 400-word fact scenario and write a detailed essay response. The Oregon bar examiners realized this and so imposed page/character limits. If you hand-wrote the exam, you had a maximum of three pages for a response; if you typed the exam, you had a maximum number of characters which worked out to almost exactly one single-spaced typed page. In such a situation, issue-spotting and rule statements are most important, while analysis will be kept to a bare minimum.

This is very similar to jurisdictions administering the Uniform Bar Exam. (In fact, Oregon has now adopted most of the UBE format.) The UBE gives you three hours to write six essays, or thirty minutes per essay. This is known as the Multistate Essay Exam or MEE.

In contrast, when I took the California bar exam, I had sixty minutes per essay and no page limit. Thus, even if you take an excruciatingly long ten minutes to read the fact scenario and outline an essay response, you still have fifty minutes to write. This is why some of the sample answers posted on the California bar website read like law review articles. With that much time issue-spotting is, of course, necessary, but analysis becomes king.

Other jurisdictions vary even more. Louisiana tests specific topics scheduled in particular blocks of time that are either two or three hours long. Within those blocks, one receives essay fact patterns which are followed by several brief questions to answer using the facts, rather than just one or two questions as in most jurisdictions. Therefore, time management is arguably more flexible within each block.

In addition to the requirements for the individual essays, determine how many essays you will be expected to answer during each segment of the bar exam. For instance, are you given a group of three essays to answer in ninety minutes or in three hours?

This is important to know because, as I will discuss in more detail later in this book, you will need to practice writing groups of essays within these longer time limits in order to ensure that you can put up with the time-pressure and endurance aspects of the bar exam. I call this "cluster practice." Furthermore, you need to practice time management to ensure that you are able to answer all the questions within the given block of time rather than spending the entire period working on a single question.

Finally, determine the percentage of your final bar exam score the essays contribute. This will help guide your studies as you move closer to the exam. You only have a limited time each day to study, so you need to prioritize your studies to give you the greatest benefit for the effort. You should take into account the value of each section of the bar exam when allocating your study efforts.

Action Step: Stop reading this book right now and go to your jurisdiction's bar website. Find the bar exam essay requirements. Write them down on a note card or sticky note and put them somewhere you will see them whenever you are working on your essays. Maybe it is on your desk, attached to your computer monitor or stuck to the front of your book of practice bar exam essays. You will have these requirements memorized in no time, but keep them visible until then.

Pillar No. 2: Issue Spotting

The second pillar for writing a good bar exam essay response is the ability to spot the issues the bar examiners want you to discuss. An "issue" is simply a topic for discussion that will be rewarded with points.

So, for example, if you discuss which of the characters in an essay's fact pattern had the most beautiful name, then you would get zero points and might be referred for psychological evaluation. But, if you discuss whether a particular statement uttered by that same character was effective to form a contract, then you will be given points.

An issue tends to be a fact in the fact pattern that will satisfy the element of a tort or crime, an act that is a possible constitutional violation, an activity of a partner in a business that is a breach of fiduciary duty, etc. Put more plainly, an issue is just whatever gives you, as the person answering the bar exam essay, an excuse to provide legal analysis.

So, how do you know what is important? How do you know what is an "issue"?

There are really three main ways you will know: (1) you will have been studying black letter law for a couple months, and so will know what is important; (2) you will have practiced various sample essays and will see exactly what bar graders believe is important; and (3) you will be told what is important by the call of the question.

Studying reveals the issues

This is probably pretty obvious.

Any element of a tort, any prong of a constitutional analysis, any element of the formation of a valid will could form the basis of an issue to discuss. You just need to learn how certain facts call out that issue and require you to discuss it.

Typically, a fact pattern will emphasize things to discuss. Keep in mind that fact patterns are fairly short, so you should assume that everything in the fact pattern raises an issue or is relevant to an issue.

This is what frustrates a lot of people. When they first begin writing practice essays, they really have not committed much of the black-letter law to memory, so they find it difficult or impossible to actually spot the issues. Just keep trying. Learn and practice at the same time. They reinforce each other and create "learning synergy."

Imagine this is taken from a wills fact pattern: "Don, the next door neighbor of Tess, a 90-year old woman with dementia, recently started visiting her every day, bringing her presents of candy and watching soap operas with her. Tess changed her will one week after Don started his visits, naming Don as her sole heir." Seems pretty obvious there is an issue of possible undue influence.

Or, imagine this taken from a torts fact pattern: "Draco was known to be a member of a tough gang. One day, he was walking down the street and walked up to Potter, a nice boy from the suburbs, and said, 'You don't belong here, you geek.' Draco then walked over to a group of friends and stared menacingly at Potter." Seems like there will be an issue about whether this was enough for an assault.

Granted, not all issues are this easy to spot, but many of them are. Just assume each sentence creates at least one issue to discuss. This will not always be true, but it is better to be suspicious than miss the issue.

Practice reveals the issues

As you practice writing essay responses, you will begin to see that certain issues are often tested together. When you notice these issue pairings, write them down somewhere and review the list once or twice per week. As your list expands, you will more easily spot issues because you will know that if you see one issue, others are likely lurking there as well.

For example, you may notice that when a civil procedure essay question involves an appeal, the issue of whether the appeal was timely is nearly always tested. Therefore, when you have an essay question mentioning an appeal, look for any facts that might lead to an argument that the appeal was untimely. Then, discuss timeliness in your essay response.

Another example comes from wills, which often tests the issue of whether a document created *after* the execution of the will somehow modifies or supersedes the will. If this issue presents itself, you will need to know the ways to test the validity of such a document (e.g., incorporation by reference, codicil, etc.) and be ready to mentally go through that list and see if any facts in the fact pattern require you to discuss those theories.

The number of permutations that can be tested on a bar exam is not infinite. You may not believe this at the start of your bar exam preparations, but it is true. In fact, many patterns repeat. If you can recognize these patterns while studying, you will be much better able to respond accurately and efficiently to essay questions.

Call of the question reveals the issues

Fortunately, you are not left entirely adrift on the issue-spotting sea because each bar exam essay question will ask you to do something specific. This is known as the call of the question.

If you understand what the call of the question is really asking you to do, it is much easier to spot issues. By carefully evaluating the call of the question, you will be able to glean a large percentage of what the examiners are looking for in a response.

Make analysis of the call of the question your first step with every practice essay so that you engrain it as part of your essay answering routine. Then, you will not forget to do it on the exam.

Let's practice this a few times, looking only at the questions with no reference to any fact patterns.

Example No. 1

If Greasy Spoon brings an action in trespass against Donald for his use of the assigned parking spaces, is Greasy Spoon likely to prevail? Discuss.

Here, you know that someone is accused of trespass. Trespass is a tort. Recall the elements of trespass and be on the lookout for facts in the fact pattern that support a conclusion that a trespass occurred.

But notice that the call also asks if Greasy Spoon is "likely to prevail." This means that you should be on the lookout for arguably unsatisfied elements of the tort as well as affirmative defenses. What are the possible defenses to trespass?

Example No. 2

What ethical violations, if any, has Jane committed? Discuss. Answer according to [your state] and ABA authorities.

Not much to go on here, other than you know it is a professional responsibility question. Be sure call to mind any common distinctions between ABA and your state's rules, and read the fact pattern with those distinctions in mind.

Example No. 3

What claims for relief might John's mother reasonably assert against Big Biz, what defenses can Big Biz reasonably raise, and what is the likely outcome on each? Discuss.

Not a ton to go on here, but it sounds like John could be a minor who got hurt by a corporation or maybe John's mother is the victim but we don't know her name for some reason. Either way, this is going to be a torts question. Therefore, likely claims for relief are negligence, strict liability, and/or products liability.

With a corporate defendant, sometimes there are employee wrongs, so vicarious liability may come in to play. There might even be a possibility of criminal liability if the fact pattern reads like a cross-over question.

Finally, the call asks for the defenses and likely outcome. Be alert for defenses and know that you will have to analyze and reach separate conclusions about each potential claim of John's mother.

Example No. 4

How successful will Cynthia be if she moves to exclude her statement to Jill under the Fifth and/or Sixth Amendments to the United States Constitution? Discuss.

Can Cynthia be convicted of murder or of any lesser-included offense? Discuss.

This two-part call tells you that this is clearly a criminal procedure / constitutional law / criminal law cross-over question.

The Fifth Amendment means *Miranda*. So, be alert for custody and interrogation, and waiver of rights. Be sure to pay close attention when Cynthia makes the "statement" referred to in the call.

The Sixth Amendment means right to counsel. When does this right attach and did it attach in the facts given to you? There will probably be arguments both ways.

Murder and lesser-included offenses mean you will have to discuss quite a few crimes and be alert for possible defenses and mitigating circumstances and defenses. I hope you know all those elements.

Conclusion

As you can see, there are various ways to learn to spot issues. These will become second nature to you as you practice them consistently in advance of the bar exam.

Pillar No. 3: Outlining and Formatting

This third pillar is all about structure. Legal writing should follow a structure. It should lead the reader step-by-step through the elements of a legal claim, discussing the relevant facts, and then coming to a conclusion.

In order to ensure your bar exam essay responses are well structured, you need to learn how to outline your answer before writing. In addition, you need to include headings to guide the bar exam grader through that structure with as little friction as possible.

Outlining your essay and formatting it are closely related. Often, the bullet points in your outline will become the headings in your essay response. Therefore, we will discuss these topics together.

Outlining

By the time you sit for the bar exam, it would be ideal if your essay outlines are nothing more than a list of bullet points that remind you what to write about. In other words, you have arrived at the point where you know the details of the law, and the "outline" serves as a checklist for writing your answer.

But, when you begin your studies, you will likely want to write more detailed outlines to make sure you have all the items down.

I will summarize the steps to creating a good outline, and then discuss them in more detail.

1. Read the call of the question.

2. Read the fact pattern, looking for facts responsive to the call and the legal theories implicated by those facts.

3. Read the call of the question again.

4. Re-read the fact pattern, and write down the legal claims/elements you need to respond to the question.

5. Read the fact pattern a third time, writing the facts you need to support the legal elements and fill in any missing legal elements.

When you first start studying for the bar exam, these five steps will take a while, maybe even ten minutes or more. But, as you become more confident with your knowledge of the law and with the essay format, you will be able to do it much more quickly. At the start of your studies, however, take as much time as you need to write a proper outline. Master the process.

Step 1 of the outline process is to perform the call of the question analysis we discussed in the prior chapter.

At **step 2**, you need to read the fact pattern, looking for facts and legal theories. For example, let's say you were asked to determine what crimes Dave could be convicted of. As you read through the fact pattern, mentally note the various crimes you see (or think you see) in the facts. Do not write anything down yet. The purpose of the first two of these five outline creation steps is to get your mind into the universe of the question, not to make any final decisions.

Step 3 requires you to re-read the call of the question. This may seem repetitive, but you must do this. Now that you have read the fact pattern once, you may notice a nuance in the call of the question that you overlooked before. In addition, re-reading the call of the question mitigates the likelihood that you will overlook or fail to discuss an important issue mentioned in the question. Unfortunately, this happens more often than you might believe.

Step 4 – re-reading the fact pattern – is very important. As you re-read the fact pattern, write down a list of all the legal claims, affirmative defenses, and issues you spot that are responsive to the call of the question. Do not list any supporting facts yet. As you write them down, try to put them in a logical order (e.g., if you are discussing the tort of negligence, list any affirmative defense to the negligence under that topic). Also, leave some space under each item you write down.

Finally, at **step 5**, re-read the fact pattern a third time, and jot down the facts you need to reference in support of the legal theories you just outlined during step 4. As you write in these supporting facts, you may also notice that you left out a sub issue or two. Fill these in as well.

It is important that you go through **all** of these steps each time you write a practice essay. The repeated reading of the fact pattern is extremely helpful to spotting all of the issues. It is a rare person who can read a fact pattern once and see everything the bar examiners are trying to get from her.

Once your outline is complete, start writing. Just remember, the outline is a guide. If, as you are writing, you realize you need to move things around to make the discussion better, then do it. But, come exam time, you should have practiced this so many times that your outlines will be concise and well-ordered, so the need for organizing on-the-fly will be much less likely.

Finally, remember that my suggested outlining steps are just that, a suggestion. If you find that a different technique works better for you, then use it.

Formatting

By formatting, I mean when to use headings or underlining in your essay response to direct the attention of the essay grader to the salient points. This is important, but also pretty easy to figure out. For some people, using headings does not come naturally, so you should practice using headings every time you write a practice essay.

First, let me say that I am not aware of any jurisdiction that actually *requires* you to use headings in your essay response. Still, effective use of headings will make it easier for an overworked bar essay grader to follow your response and give you a higher grade. Therefore, I recommend you use headings.

The most important headings are those that break your essay response into its main parts. For example, pretend you were responding to the following call of the question:

How successful will Cynthia be if she moves to exclude her statement to Jill under the Fifth and/or Sixth Amendments to the United States Constitution? Discuss.

Can Cynthia be convicted of murder or of any lesser-included offense? Discuss.

You would need two main subject headings, similar to:

I. Cynthia's Motion to Exclude and
II. Will Cynthia be convicted of murder or other crimes?

I recommend using roman numerals or ALL-CAPS to set these main headings apart from any subheadings you intend to use. This makes them stand out strongly from the rest of your text and alerts the grader you are switching main topics.

Under each of these, you would likely want to use appropriate subheadings. For this call of the question, some likely subheadings might be:

Exclusion under the Fifth Amendment
Exclusion under the Sixth Amendment
Murder
Voluntary Manslaughter
Involuntary Manslaughter

As subheadings, these should *not* be preceded by roman numerals or be in ALL-CAPS, but should be more subtle, and clearly encompassed within the main heading. You might choose to indent or underline them.

Compare that to the following call of the question:

What ethical violations, if any, has Jane committed? Discuss. Answer according to [your state] and ABA authorities.

Because the entire question is about ethical violations, there is really no need for a main subject heading to regurgitate that for the grader. Instead, I would recommend using headings for each ethical violation you find in the fact pattern, and then subheadings identifying ABA and state variations, if applicable. Something like this:

Duty of Competence

ABA

State

Duty of Candor

ABA

State

No Sex with Clients

ABA

State

Another example is a call of the question asking what claims a plaintiff could bring against a defendant based on the fact pattern. There, you would certainly want to list each claim as a main heading. You may or may not want to list each of the elements of the claim as subheadings when you discuss them.

There is no one right way to do headings. I recommend that you review sample essay answers from your jurisdiction to see how headings are used in those answers. If headings seem to be everywhere, incorporate lots of headings in your responses. If headings are sparingly used, then your responses should be similarly austere.

Conclusion

The best way to learn how to outline essay responses and to use headings is to practice. But, before you rush off to practice these things, we need to discuss essay analysis.

Pillar No. 4: Analysis

I have saved the best and most important thing for last. Without good analysis in your essay response, you have little chance of receiving a passing score.

Before we get into the details of bar exam analysis, let's think back to law school essay exams. As you will recall, there was usually some amount of uncertainty or ambiguity when responding to a law school essay question. There were usually facts or theories supporting both sides of an argument, such as a finding of liability versus no liability or a violation of due process versus no violation. The point is that you were being tested on how you analyzed facts in light of the applicable law, not how well you argued a single position.

It is typically the same in the bar exam. You will find yourself using phrases like "it is likely that a court would find x, but it is also possible that defendant will prevail because of the affirmative defense of y" or "under these facts, it is not likely a court would find a contract was formed, but if it was formed, then Mr. D breached the contract when he did x, y and z."

The quality of your legal analysis is the most important factor in determining whether you will pass the essay portion of the bar exam. The entire point of the test is to ensure that members of the bar can perform basic legal analysis to assist clients and avoid malpractice lawsuits.

You must know how to analyze. Therefore you must know IRAC.

IRAC

IRAC is an acronym standing for Issue, Rule, Application/Analysis, and Conclusion. It is the structure you will use to analyze each bar exam essay fact pattern.

Some people hate IRAC, and there are some bar exam preparation courses that actually suggest another method. It does not matter what you think about IRAC – it is the analytical standard for bar exams. Do not question it. Learn it and use it.

Let's review each part of the IRAC format so we have the same baseline understanding.

Issue

Your IRAC analysis should start with a statement of the issues or legal questions to which you will respond in the remainder of your essay. However, do not be as formal as you were in law school. Instead of something like "whether Doug is liable for negligence," You can use a heading like: **Was Doug negligent?** or **Will David's confession be excluded from evidence?** An initial heading frames your response, and lets the grader know what to expect.

Rule

The Rule section of an IRAC follows the issue heading and should give a summary of the applicable rule or rules of law. To continue with our negligence example, you could write something like: *"In order for Doug to be found negligent, he must have owed a duty to Paul, breached that duty, Paul must have suffered harm, and Doug's breach of duty must be the actual and proximate cause of that harm."*

Obviously, the rule statement or statements you provide are dependent on the specificity of the call of the question and the facts in the fact pattern.

It is important to get the rule statement correct because it will guide your analysis of the facts in the fact pattern.

Application/Analysis

The Application (or Analysis) section of an IRAC essay response applies the rule or rules of law to the specific facts of the issue at hand. This is the most important section of your essay response. This is where you get to show the grader that you are capable of performing legal analysis and therefore worthy of bar admission.

It is important that your analysis stays on target, applying all relevant facts to the legal rules. You will need to explain why a particular rule applies or does not apply to the given facts. Most of the time, you will need to argue both sides of an issue. For example, "In light of these facts, Doug was likely negligent, but could escape liability if fact x is proven because it would support his assertion of affirmative defense y."

Conclusion

If the Rule and Analysis sections of your IRAC were done well, the Conclusion section is almost perfunctory.

There are potentially three areas of your essay where you will write a conclusion. You may need to write sub-conclusions at the completion of each sub-analysis in your essay. If the essay response is very short, there may only be a single conclusion. If it is a longer, multi-part essay, you will reach several sub-conclusions and perhaps one overall conclusion.

It is less important to get the "correct" conclusion, than simply to come to a conclusion that is supported by the facts as you have applied them to a rule of law. Often, bar exam questions are written such that you could justifiably reach one of two or three conclusions.

Action Step: Stop reading this book and go to your jurisdiction's website and read a few sample essay questions and answers. See how IRAC is the typical format for the answer? Ask yourself, how well was IRAC applied in the model answer? How could it have been improved? (Note: If your jurisdiction does not provide model bar essay responses, go to the California bar website and search for "past exams" to see numerous model answers.)

Conclusion

If you have had trouble with IRAC in law school, now is the time to figure it out. During your first few weeks of essay practice, be deliberate in applying IRAC. When you review model answers, be hypercritical of your application of IRAC. If you are having a lot of trouble, try rewriting a practice essay two or three times until you get it.

How to Practice

Now that we have discussed the four pillars of writing a passing bar exam essay, there is little left to do except practice writing essays.

Practice is the most important thing you can do to pass the bar exam. Practice is important because it is an active form of learning, as opposed to the relatively passive form of rote memorization of black letter law. It forces you to engage the material by responding to it and then reviewing and learning from your mistakes and omissions. Active practice is part of having a growth mindset as opposed to a fixed mindset.

This chapter is a summary of what I believe is the most effective way to practice for the bar essays. It is the method I used both times I took the bar exam, and it is the method I recommend to students I have tutored for the bar exam. This method is not, of course, the *only* way to practice for the essay portion of the bar exam. So, feel free to modify it as necessary to fit your needs.

This practice method lasts for ten weeks because most full-time bar preparation programs start ten weeks before the bar exam. Typically, you follow a preset study program for eight weeks, and then you have the final two weeks before the bar exam to study on your own.

If you are studying over a longer or shorter period of time than ten weeks, you will need to adjust the schedule accordingly. If you would like a PDF copy of this schedule to hang on your wall or to makes notes on, you can download a copy at *barexammind.com/essays*.

Weeks 1-3

During the first three weeks of bar exam preparations, your main assignment is to stay on task and avoid being overwhelmed with your bar prep. With respect to essay preparation, the goals are to get comfortable writing essays, including the basics of timing and structure.

When you write the practice essays assigned by your bar prep program, set a timer for the length of time allowed by your jurisdiction, and then write your essay responses. Go ahead and use notes or bar review outlines during these initial weeks of practice.

At this stage of your preparations, it is not about what you know; it is about learning the format and the process. If you are still writing when your essay timer sounds, keep writing until you have written as complete a response as you are capable of at this time. At this point, it is important to understand the time limits, but do not abide by them. You need to learn how to write the essays; speed and efficiency will come later.

The most important thing to do during these first weeks is to evaluate your essay responses in order to understand what is going right and what is going wrong. After you complete a sample essay response, spend as much time as you need reading through the model answer and determining what issues you missed and where your IRAC was weak or broke down. If the model answer referred to a legal concept you do not understand, then go to your bar review materials and read about that concept.

Don't try to memorize everything you missed at this point, just review it so that you are familiar with it. Bar exam preparation is a cumulative process, so do not worry if you missed several issues or wrote a terrible analysis. You are just at the start of your prep.

If you are assigned so many practice essays that you feel you cannot do a thorough review of each essay after you write it, then I recommend skipping some of the assigned essays at this point. During these first weeks, the *quality* of your practice is more important than the *quantity* of your practice. You can use the essays you skip now for your review during the final two weeks before the bar exam.

Weeks 4-6

During these next three weeks, you need to tighten up your response technique. First, get your timing down. Set a timer for each essay for the maximum time allowed by your jurisdiction. When the timer sounds, stop writing. Ideally, by the end of these three weeks, you will be able to finish each essay with a few minutes to spare.

Second, from this point forward, you are not to use notes when writing your essay responses. Do your best from memory. Yes, you will miss some points or maybe even a lot of points, but that is okay. You still have more than a month until the bar exam. If you continue to use your notes while practicing, they will become a crutch, and it will be difficult to trust yourself when writing. You need to be confident on the bar exam, and the sooner you stop using notes, the more quickly your confidence will increase.

Third, review each practice essay response as you have been. The only difference now is when you find that you have missed an issue or botched a portion of your analysis, rewrite it. This rewriting will allow you to get the feel for a better analysis. It will give you practice writing an essay as good as the model essay. It will also lead you to a better understanding of the essay writing process.

Weeks 7-8

Your essay response technique should all be coming together now. Maybe you still have some weak subjects, but your ability to write a response within the appropriate time and of the appropriate length should be well developed.

To the extent that you are very confident with certain subjects, you can probably stop writing full essay responses for those subjects. Instead, just outline the essay response, checking it against the model answer to make sure that you are spotting all of the issues. Focus the majority of your time and energy writing essays for the topics you feel are your weakest.

Weeks 9-10

The final two weeks before the bar exam is when you get entire days to study as you wish. No more lectures, no more scheduled work. This is when you solidify your knowledge and get rid of as many weak spots as possible.

As far as the essays go, I recommend that you do some **cluster practice**, which means writing groups of essays under timed conditions.

For example, if your jurisdiction requires examinees to respond to three essays in ninety minutes, then you should practice responding to three essays in ninety minutes. Select three essays, set a timer for ninety minutes and write.

Do this as many times as you need to get the timing down. Practice moving on to the next essay after thirty minutes *no matter what*. If you are still working on the response at minute twenty-nine, whip out a quick conclusion and go to the next essay. If you get bogged down on an essay during the bar exam for sixty minutes, you will not be able to write good responses to the other two essays and the results could be disastrous.

In addition to cluster practice, be sure to do a full-blown practice exam. If you are part of a bar review program, the program probably has such an exam scheduled. If not, create one for yourself.

Try to do your essay practice exam on the same day of the week as you will be taking it during the real bar exam. It is important to match the day of the week with the format so that your mind and body synchronize their abilities with the correct days of the week. Furthermore, find out the approximate start time of your state's bar exam. Be sure that you start and stop your practice examination within those time parameters so that the practice session is as realistic as possible.

After you have completed sufficient cluster practice to get the timing down and have taken one full-blown practice exam, you may not need to write any more practice essays. *Only you will know whether this is true.* If you feel you are prepared to write your essays come exam day, then spend your time outlining practice essays and checking those outlines against the model answers. Use the time you would have spent writing full-length practice essays to prepare for other portions of the bar exam or to work on memorizing any areas of law with which you are having difficulty.

Essay practice checklist

Above, I explained my ten-week practice schedule for bar exam essays. It might be helpful for you to have a checklist of steps to follow with each individual essay that you practice so you can be sure to do each of them.

Here are the steps I recommend:

1. Choose a practice question
2. Set a timer for the jurisdictional maximum time
3. Read the call of question
4. Read the fact pattern
5. Re-read the call of question
6. Re-read the fact pattern and fill in outline headings and subheadings based on the legal issues you spot

7. Re-read the call of question and fact pattern and add the supporting facts to your outline

8. Write the essay

9. Compare your response to model answer

10. What issues did you miss? Why did you miss them? What facts triggered the need to discuss these issues?

11. Was your analysis complete? If not, what did you leave out? Why did you leave it out? Did you miss a critical fact, or is it simply so early in your studies that you have not learned that concept?

12. What went well with this practice essay? What do you need to improve?

A copy of this checklist will be included with the PDF essay schedule you can download at *barexammind.com/essays*.

Additional Essay Tips

When I have helped students with their essay writing, I have noticed some common problems. So, I have developed a list of tips to help solve those problems. Not all of these approaches will work for everyone.

Canned responses

As you practice and review multiple essays, you will learn that certain phrases or concepts get repeated. It is very helpful to have a paragraph or two memorized about these concepts so that you can open your essay with it.

For example, let's say you are responding to an Evidence essay. Perhaps you have been asked to determine whether certain statements will be admitted at trial. You could simply analyze each statement, going through the various steps, applying the hearsay rule and exceptions, etc. This is fine, and if you do a good job on the analysis, it should be sufficient to write a passing answer.

But, if you have the time and the space, why not begin with a short canned paragraph about the basic steps of evidence analysis. This will give the reader a clue that you understand what you need to do, and it will help you get warmed up. You could write something like the following:

"Under the Federal Rules of Evidence, evidence is admissible if it is logically and legally relevant. Relevant evidence is evidence having any tendency to make the existence of a fact that is of consequence to the determination of an action more probable than it would be without the evidence. Relevant evidence is admissible unless excluded by another rule of evidence, a statute or the Constitution. Irrelevant evidence is not admissible."

While not all topics lend themselves to a canned general introductory paragraph, where possible, create and memorize such a paragraph to insert at the start of each essay. By doing this, you ease your way into the answer and give the essay grader a sense that you truly understand the context of your answer. Plus, you begin your essay with "magic words" or "terms of art" which will resonate with the grader.

Here is a sample opening paragraph that could be useful when responding to a contracts essay question:

"Before analyzing the validity and effect of the contract between X and Y, it is important to determine whether to apply the common law or the UCC. The UCC applies to the sale of goods, whereas the common law of contracts generally applies to contracts for services, real estate, insurance, intangible assets, and employment. If the contract is for both the sale of goods and for services, the dominant element (or gravamen) in the contract controls."

Some examples of topics that might lend themselves to a canned paragraph include:

1. Personal jurisdiction with minimum contacts analysis
2. Subject matter jurisdiction
3. Summary of elements of a valid trust
4. Basics of intentional torts
5. Summary of *mens rea, actus reus*, concurrence and harm
6. Standing to sue
7. Summary of the elements of negligence

Double-check essay facts

Another issue I have noticed with certain students is missing (or maybe forgetting) a critical fact while writing their essay response. Sometimes, a forgotten fact can have minor consequences, but other times it will totally derail your analysis and have a jarring effect on the reader.

I suggest that after you create your initial essay outline, you re-read the fact pattern of the essay one more time before you start writing your response. This will increase the odds you will not miss the important facts.

Some examples of facts to double-check include:

1. Who is offering the testimony?
2. What are the terms of the lease?
3. When did the event occur?

4. Where did the event occur?

5. Who made the statement to whom?

6. Is the asset held jointly or in one name only?

7. Was the agreement written or oral?

8. Does the amount of time between events x and y implicate a rule of law or affirmative defense?

Obviously, the list could be extended for quite some length. The point is that in a bar exam essay, *it is often the little facts that make the biggest difference.*

As you practice writing essay responses, be on the lookout for any facts you tend to miss. If you notice a pattern of errors, ensure that whenever you have an essay that tends to contain those sorts of facts, that you are extra-cautious when writing your response.

While it is inevitable that at least some of your essay responses will have imperfections, self-knowledge and awareness will help make your essay responses as strong as possible.

How to target your weak subjects

By the final week or so before the bar exam, it is likely you will have a good general understanding of the majority of the bar exam material.

You will also have a few weak spots; I know I did. *(Yeah, I'm thinking about you, community property!)* Be sure to target those weak spots by writing a few sample essays in full.

You can even re-write essays you did earlier in your bar prep. This is a good test to see how much you have improved. This will help you hone your analytical skills for that topic, and it will allow you to keep up your timing practice.

I think a good system for targeting weak areas is to review flash cards focusing on the weakness, answer 5-10 MBE questions on the same subject matter (if applicable), and then write an essay about that topic. Once you review your answer to the essay, skim your full bar exam outline (or equivalent) for that subject area or sub-subject area.

Practice under exam-like conditions

I suggest that you set aside at least one block of cluster practice for this. Locate a place where there will be a sizeable number of people who will be making at least some noise but where you will not likely be interrupted by someone speaking to you. This is what it will be like when you are taking the actual bar exam. Ideal places include a busy public library or a coffee shop.

Then, go to your chosen place and write a block of essays under timed conditions. If possible, try to do this on two or three separate occasions. Of course, be sure to do it at the time of day when you would actually be doing the same thing for the bar examination.

If your bar has odd rules for its exam, be sure to incorporate them into your practice. For example, the Virginia Bar requires applicants take the bar examination wearing business attire. How would you like to fail because you weren't comfortable taking a test in a coat and tie (men) or wearing a tailored skirt or suit or heels (women)? Do not let yourself fail for a foolish reason and for lack of practice.

Finally, if you intend to wear earplugs when taking the bar exam, make sure you wear them during at least some of your practice sessions. I recommend earplugs and used them myself both times I took the bar exam. The feeling of them in your ears does take some getting used to, so I do not recommend using them for the first time on bar exam day.

Suggested Approach for Bar Exam Essay Day

Now that you know how to write good bar exam essay responses, the only thing left is to take the real test. When responding to bar exam essays on test day, you need to make sure that you manage your time so that you can respond to each essay as completely as possible. Because you have been practicing doing this, you should be quite good at time management.

In this chapter, I outline a simple approach to ensure you achieve the maximum points possible on your essays in the amount of time you have to respond to them. If this approach appeals to you, I suggest you practice it at least twice while doing your cluster practice.

On the bar exam, you will be required to respond to a group of essays during a predetermined period of time. For example, you may be assigned three essays to write during a ninety-minute block of time (or, if you are in California, a three-hour block of time).

The best way to approach these essays is to **answer them in order of your competence** on each topic, rather than automatically answering them in the order in which they are assigned.

Even though you should have studied all possible topics, it is typical for most people to have some subjects in which they are stronger and others in which they are weaker. When responding to bar exam essays, I recommend you respond to the essay you feel most confident about, then the next most confident, and finally the least confident.

By doing this, your first essay will be quite good. This will give you confidence as you move forward and respond to the remaining essays. When you start responding to your second essay, the confidence you felt during the first one will carry over.

By the time you start your third essay, you will have written two good responses. Your confidence in those responses will help you write a better essay answer than if you had started with the weakest topic first.

Example

I will use my experience with the California bar exam as an example of how this process works.

When I took the bar exam, the second essay section had essays with the following topics in the following order:

- Trusts/Wills
- Community Property
- Corporations/Professional Responsibility

Now, if I were to order them just based on the general topic, I would have responded to Corporations/Professional Responsibility first, Trusts/Wills second, and Community Property third.

But, you should not decide just based on the topic.

Be sure to analyze the call of the question and skim the fact pattern to see how complicated your response will be. Maybe the general topic is a weak one for you, but the specific area being tested is a strong-suit.

So, in the example above, the Trusts/Wills question was about formation and revocation of a trust and whether a valid will had been formed. These were topics I was pretty good at. The Corporations/PR question seemed extremely complex, and did not seem like something I wanted to attack first. And, the Community Property question was awful, as I had suspected.

So, I reordered my response and answered the Trusts/Wills question first, Corporations/PR second, and Community Property last. I wrote a great response to the first essay, and felt strong as I went through the other two essays.

Conclusion

If you think this might be helpful to you, be sure to practice it. Have a friend or study buddy select three non-overlapping essay questions for you. Then, put aside the normal time to respond to the questions, and go for it.

Just make sure that you do not spend more than the maximum amount of time on each essay. In other words, if you have to write three essays in ninety minutes, do not spend more than thirty minutes on a single response.

Conclusion

The process of writing good bar exam essays is not a difficult one, but it does require commitment and a significant investment of time. If you engage in consistent essay practice and thorough self-assessment of your practice essays, you will be writing good essays within a short period of time.

The important thing is to approach your essay practice with a growth mindset and with the confidence that you will improve with additional practice.

Bar Exam Resources

If you would like additional information and strategies for bar exam success, please check out my blog at BarExamMind.com. There, you will find helpful articles and product reviews. You can also sign up for the Bar Exam Mind newsletter and get access to my popular bar exam outlines.

And, don't forget about the other books in the "Pass the Bar Exam" series:

Bar Exam Basics: A Roadmap to Bar Exam Success

Bar Exam Mind: A Strategy Guide for an Anxiety-Free Bar Exam

The Bar Exam Mind Bar Exam Journal

For even more resources, be sure to visit *BarExamMind.com*. While you are there, be sure to sign up for my email newletter.

Contact Me

I would love to hear what you thought about this book. You can let me know either by leaving a review on your favorite book review site or platform or by contacting me directly at *barexammind.com/contact.*

78758133R00069